# Lingo Dingo and the Welsh chef

Written by Mark Pallis

Illustrated by James Cottell

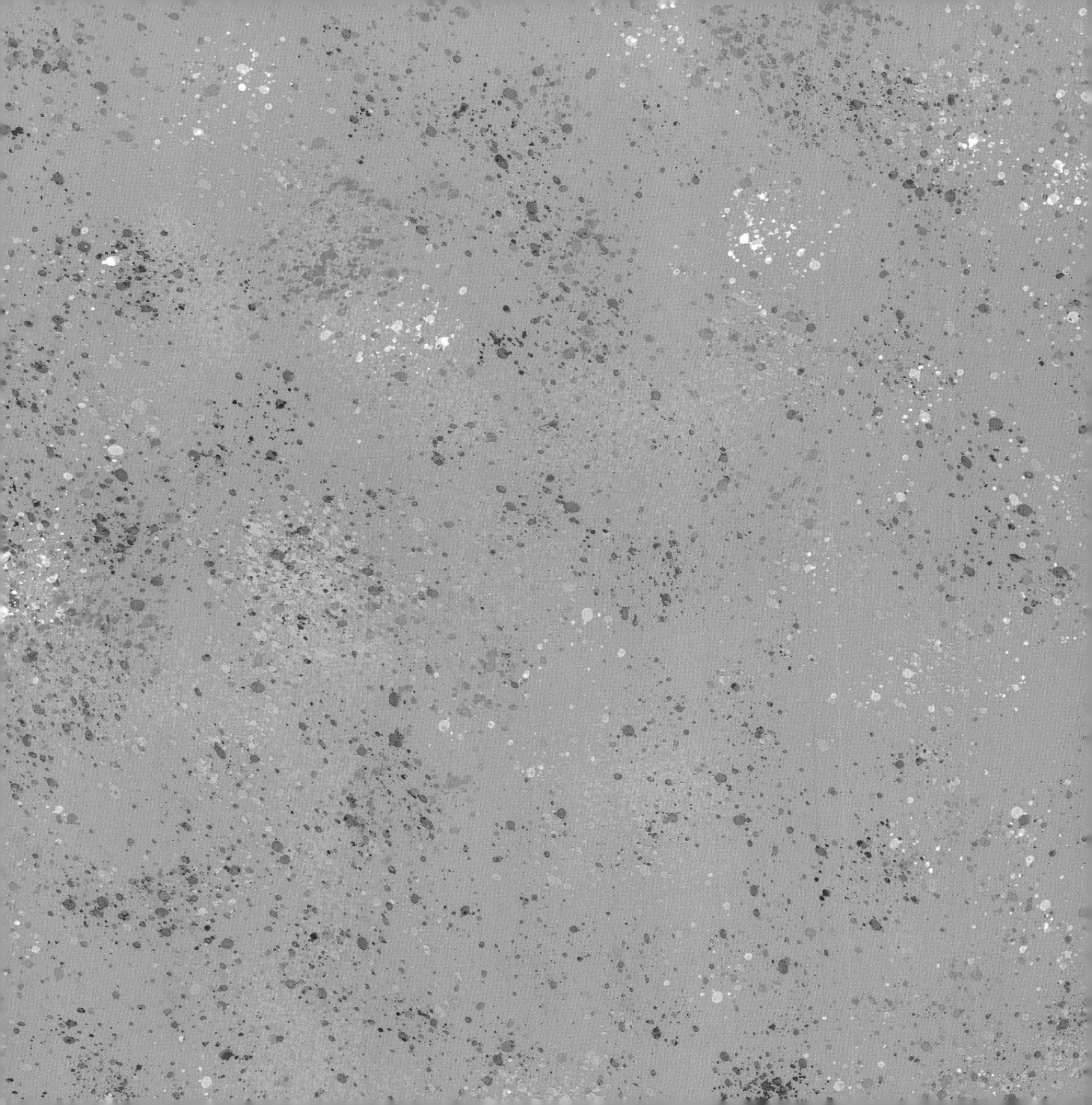

For my awesome sons- MP

For Leo and Juniper - JC

LINGO DINGO AND THE WELSH CHEF



Story edited by Natascha Biebow, Blue Elephant Storyshaping
First Printing, 2022
ISBN: 978-1-915337-36-8
NeuWestendPress.com

# Lingo Dingo and the Welsh chef

Written by Mark Pallis
Illustrated by James Cottell

NEU WESTEND
— PRESS —

This is Lingo. She's a Dingo and she loves helping.

Anyone. Anytime. Anyhow.

Lingo often helps her stylish neighbour Gunther, who lives by himself next door. She does a few jobs and has a nice chat. It makes Gunther feel good and it makes Lingo feel good too.

One day, Lingo arranged a special birthday party for Gunther. She even ordered a cake from a famous Welsh chef.

There was a knock at the door, "It must be the cake!" said Lingo. But it was a monkey.

"Helô. Fy enw i ydy Cogydd Glyn. Mae gen i broblem," he said.

*Oh no. I can't speak Welsh yet,* thought Lingo. *Maybe 'Helô' is like 'Hello'.*

**Helô** = Hello; **Fy enw i ydy** = My name is; **Mae gen i broblem** = I have a problem

"Helô," said Lingo. Chef Glyn replied slowly,
"Mae'n ddrwg gen i. Ni allaf wneud y gacen ben-blwydd."

"I don't understand," said Lingo. "But let me guess. You want..."

**mae'n ddrwg gen i** = I am sorry; **Ni allaf wneud** = I cannot make;
**y gacen ben-blwydd** = the birthday cake

**troli** = a trolley; **gercin** = gherkin; **balwnau**= balloons; **na** = no

“Mae fy ffwrn wedi torri,” explained Chef.

“Gaf i ddefnyddio popty ti?”

*Chef’s oven must be broken* thought Lingo. “I know! Let’s bake the cake together,” she said.

**mae fy ffwrn wedi torri** = my oven is broken;
**Gaf i ddefnyddio popty ti?** = can I use your oven?

Chef tapped his wrist. “Faint o’r gloch ydy hi?
Naw o’r gloch? Deg o’r gloch” he asked.

Lingo pointed
at her watch.

“Un ar ddeg o’r gloch? Gadewch i ni ddechrau! Cyflym!” ”
They only had one hour until the party.

**Faint o’r gloch ydy hi?** = what time is it?; **Naw o’r gloch** = nine o’clock; **Deg o’r gloch** = ten o’clock;
**Un ar ddeg o’r gloch** = eleven o’clock; **Gadewch i ni ddechrau** = let’s go; **Cyflym** = quick

Chef Glyn and Lingo whizzed around the kitchen:

**Ffedog i ti** = an apron for you; **Chwisg** = a whisk;
**Powlen gymysgu** = a mixing bowl

"Pasiwch y menyn, siwgr, wyau a blawd i mi os gwelwch yn dda," said Chef.

Lingo wasn't sure what those words meant, so she just grabbed fish, coffee and onions instead.

"Pysgod, coffi a nionod. Ffiaidd!" laughed Chef.

**Pasiwch** = pass; **menyn** = butter; **siwgr** = the sugar; **wyau** = the eggs; **blawd** = flour; **os gwelwch yn dda** = please; **Pysgod** = fish; **coffi** = coffee; **nionod** = onions; **Ffiaidd** = disgusting

Chef plopped sugar, butter, eggs and flour into a bowl. "So that's what 'menyn, siwgr, wyau a blawd' means!" laughed Lingo.

"Rwy'n cymysgu, ti'n cymysgu, ni'n cymysgu," said Chef and together they began to mix the cake.

**Rwy'n cymysgu** = I mix; **ti'n cymysgu** = you mix; **ni'n cymysgu** = we mix

"Yn olaf, powdr pobi. Dwy lwyaid ," said Chef. Lingo guessed 'powdr pobi' meant baking powder, but how much?

Before she could ask, Chef hurried away, saying, "Esgusodwch fi, mae angen i mi droethi."

Lingo laughed, "I can guess what 'droethi' means!"

**Yn olaf** = finally; **powdr pobi** = baking powder; **Dwy lwyaid** = two spoonfulls; **Esgusodwch fi** = excuse me; **Esgusodwch fi, mae angen i mi droethi** = I need to do a wee wee

*I wonder if this is too much?* thought Lingo as she added ten spoonfulls of 'powdr pobi' to the mix.

She carefully put everything into the oven and before long, a sweet cakey smell filled the kitchen.

**powdr pobi** = baking powder

"Beth ddigwyddodd? Mae'n enfawr!" said Chef.

Lingo realised she had added too much baking powder.

"Sorry," she said sheepishly.

**Beth ddigwyddodd** = what happened; **Mae'n enfawr** = it's huge

**Trychineb** = disaster

"I know what will make you feel better," said Lingo, kindly. "Eat this 'gercin'!"

"Ffiaidd. Mae'n gas gen i gercinau." said Chef.

They were running out of time.

**Ffiaidd** = disgusting; **Mae'n gas gen i gercinau** = I hate gherkins

“I’ve got it! Gunther loves hats, so let’s turn the cakey mess into a hat cake! ” said Lingo.

First she shaped the cake, then she filled balloons with icing.

Next came the best part: POP! POP! POP!

It was a messy job but in the end, the cake looked fantastic.

"Coch, oren, melyn, gwyrdd, glas. Ffantastig!" said Chef.

**coch** = red; **noren** = orange; **melyn** = yellow; **vgwyrdd** = green; **glas** = blue; **ffantastig** = fantastic

There was a knock at the door.
"Y drws!" said Chef.
It was Gunther, and he was wearing his special hat!

"Thankyou. This makes me feel so special," said Gunther.
"You are special," replied Lingo.

**Y drws** = the door

**Pen-blwydd hapus i ti** = happy birthday to you

"Chwythwch!" said Chef.

Gunther blew out all the candles in one puff and everyone tucked in.

**Chwythwch** = blow

"Rwy'n bwyta, ti'n bwyta, e'n bwyta, hi'n bwyta, nhw'n bwyta."

laughed Chef.

"Ni'n bwyta!" added Lingo proudly.

**rwy'n bwyta** = I eat; **ti'n bwyta** = you eat; **e'n bwyta** = he eats;
**hi'n bwyta** = she eats; **nhw'n bwyta** = they eat; **ni'n bwyta** = we eat

Lingo, Gunther and Chef watched the sun go down.

"Rwy'n hapus,

ti'n hapus.

Rydyn ni gyd yn hapus," said Chef.

**rwy'n hapus** = I am happy; **ti'n hapus** = you are happy; **rydyn ni gyd yn hapus**= we are all happy

Baking a cake, helping a friend,
learning a new language... what a day!

But now it was time for bed. It was time to dream
about all the fun things that might happen tomorrow.

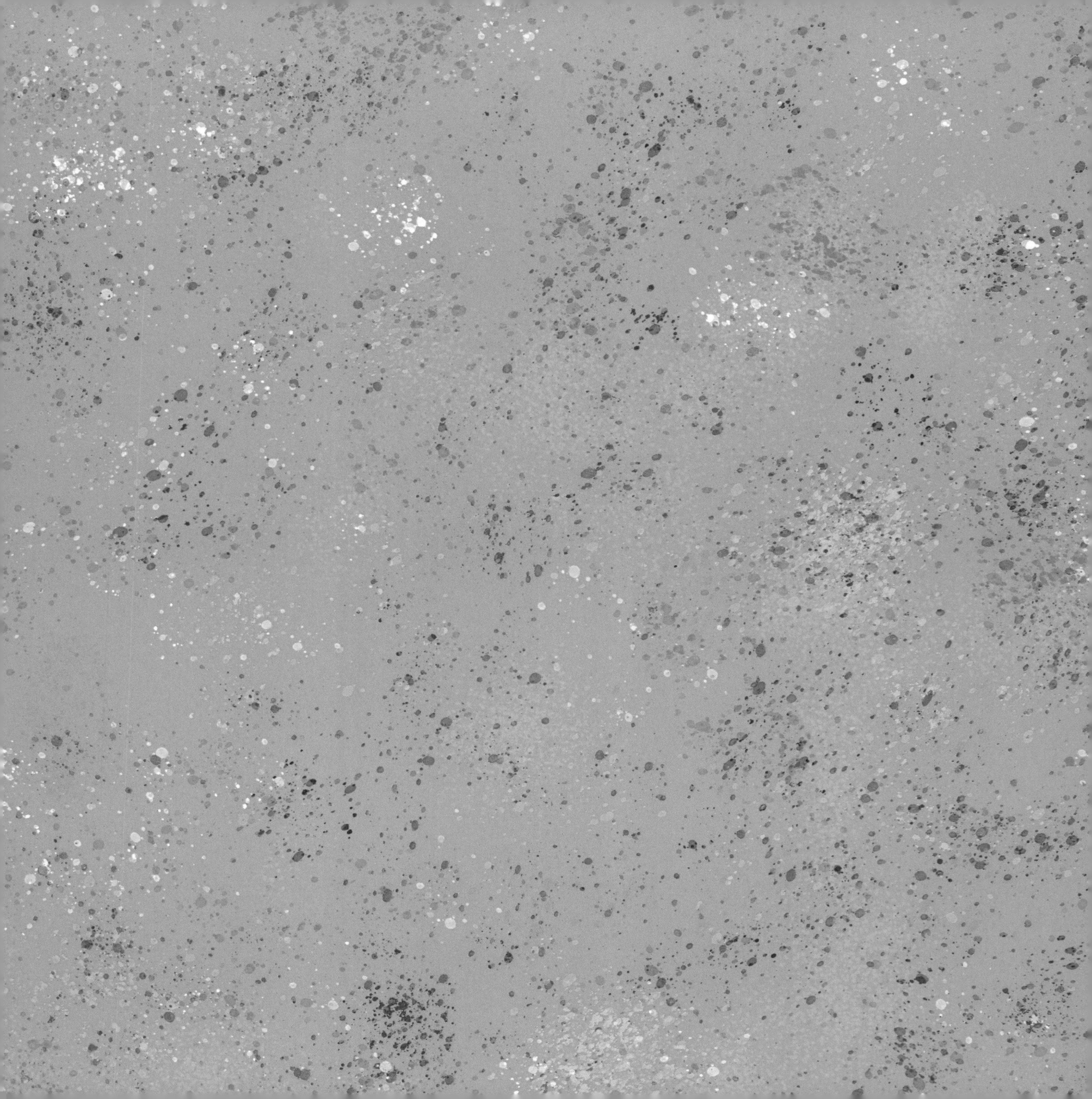

## Learning to love languages

An additional language opens a child's mind, broadens their horizons and enriches their emotional life. Research has shown that the time between a child's birth and their sixth or seventh birthday is a "golden period" when they are most receptive to new languages. This is because they have an in-built ability to distinguish the sounds they hear and make sense of them. The Story-powered Language Learning Method taps into these natural abilities.

## How the Story-powered language learning Method works

We create an emotionally engaging and funny story for children and adults to enjoy together, just like any other picture book. Studies show that social interaction, like enjoying a book together, is critical in language learning.

Through the story, we introduce a relatable character who speaks only in the new language. This helps build empathy and a positive attitude towards people who speak different languages. These are both important aspects in laying the foundations for lasting language acquisition in a child's life.

As the story progresses, the child naturally works with the characters to discover the meanings of a wide range of fun new words. Strategic use of humour ensures that this subconscious learning is rewarded with laughter; the child feels good and the first seeds of a lifelong love of languages are sown.

**For more information and free learning resources visit www.neuwestendpress.com**